# CHEERFUL
## IN 3½ MONTHS

# PREFACE

I become cheerful whenever the robins visit my garden in the autumn. I become cheerful from the color of a blooming poppy. I become cheerful whenever my little girl dresses herself in clothes with lots of pink, stripes and little dots.

Ask anyone what makes them happy and they will tell you – after first perhaps mentioning all the usual X-rated stuff – that it's the little things that matter. Peeling a tangerine and leaving its skin intact. Walking through snow as it crunches underfoot. The smell of fresh coffee in the morning. Then there's the pyromaniac who feels – deep down in his heart – more cheerful the moment he is lighting the match than when he is watching the fire he started. I am talking about such things as that little skip you sometimes feel in your heart, that little fairy whispering 'yes' into your ear, those two hedgehogs rubbing their spikes against each other.

Everyone has a day when darkness turns into sunshine. When someone lets you take shelter under their umbrella. When you smell some freshly sizzling bacon. When you discover an extra roll of toilet paper just when you thought you'd run out.

That is why we created this book. Now you can be your own magic fairy and give yourself those special moments of cheer. One assignment a day for 3.5 months. It may not be much but it's happiness.

Gerard Janssen

ST

# 1 MONTH

# PHOTOCOPY YOUR BUTT

- DAY 1 -

**PRACTICE DOING A WHEELIE ON YOUR BIKE**

- DAY 2 -

**RENT A METAL DETECTOR AND SEARCH FOR LOST TREASURES**

- DAY 3 -

# KEEP PAINTING DOTS ON A GIANT CANVAS UNTIL IT'S COMPLETELY COVERED

- DAY 4 -

# NAME ALL OF YOUR FAVORITE BODY PARTS

- DAY 5 -

**BECOME ONE WITH THE WAVES**

- DAY 6 -

# SEND A GIFT TO A STRANGER

- DAY 8 -

# BECOME A PERFECTIONIST

- [ ] SET ALL YOUR CLOCKS TO EXACTLY THE SAME TIME. CHECK BY USING AN ALARM CLOCK

- [ ] POLISH YOUR SHOES

- [ ] GET TO AN APPOINTMENT ON TIME. DON'T BE A SECOND EARLY OR LATE

- [ ] MAKE A SANDWICH, COVER EVERY INCH

- [ ] SHARPEN YOUR PENCILS

- [ ] BUILD TIDY STACKS OF EVERYTHING AROUND YOU

- [ ] PICK YOUR WORDS CAREFULLY (NO BULLSHIT)

# HAIRDRESSER

**VISIT THE HAIRDRESSER AND VISIT ANOTHER ONE STRAIGHT AFTER. REPEAT THIS FOUR TIMES**

- DAY 10 -

**TAKE A SHOVEL FROM THE SHED**

**TAKE A RAKE FROM THE SHED**

**MAKE A SHOVEL RAKE**

**BURY THE HANDLE THAT IS LEFT**

- DAY 11 -

# FACE YOUR FEAR OF THE UNKNOWN

- DAY 12 -

## HAVE A PERFECTLY ILLOGICAL DAY

- I WILL NOT PUT CHEESE IN MY SANDWICH BECAUSE I LOVE CHEESE
- I WILL VISIT THE BUTCHER JUST BECAUSE IT 'FEELS GOOD'
- I DON'T BELIEVE IN ALIENS FROM OUTER SPACE. THAT'S WHY I BURIED LOVE LETTERS TO THEM IN MY BACKYARD
- I NEED SIX SCREWS. THAT'S WHY I BOUGHT 600
- I FELT COLD SO I TURNED OFF THE TV

- DAY 14 -

**IF NO ONE IS WATCHING, HOP LIKE A BLACKBIRD. BUT IF PEOPLE TAKE NOTICE, ACT SENSIBLY AND WALK LIKE A STARLING, ONE FOOT AT A TIME.**

- DAY 17 -

**STAY OUTSIDE AS MUCH AS POSSIBLE**

FOREST

- DAY 19 -

**WALK AROUND REACHING OUT**

# SAY SOME- THING TO ME

- DAY 20 -

# ASK A STRANGER WHAT HE/SHE THINKS OF YOU

- ☐ BEAUTIFUL
- ☐ ATTRACTIVE
- ☐ INTRIGUING
- ☐ ASTOUNDING
- ☐ STUBBORN
- ☐ CHARMING
- ☐ GOLD, PURE GOLD

# BE YOUR FAVORITE PIECE OF PIE

- DAY 22 -

# PAINT A PAIR OF JEANS AND A T-SHIRT ON YOUR BODY AND PAY A VISIT TO A NUDIST CAMPSITE

- DAY 24 -

USE DUCT TAPE TO ATTACH BINOCULARS BACKWARDS TO YOUR FACE SO EVERYTHING SEEMS REALLY SMALL AND FAR AWAY

- DAY 25 -

## ORDER AN IMPOSSIBLE PIZZA

- DAY 26 -

# LEARN THE ARABIC ALPHABET

*

\* RHUBARB

- DAY 27 -

**FIND A GIANT CARDBOARD BOX AND WEAR IT WHILE WALKING FROM ONE SIDE OF THE CITY TO THE OTHER. GET PEOPLE TO HELP YOU OUT**

- DAY 28 -

**CATCH A FLY OR BEETLE AND STUDY IT UNDER A MAGNIFYING GLASS**

- DAY 29 -

**EAT SOMETHING YOU'VE NEVER EATEN BEFORE**

- DAY 30 -

**GIVE YOUR CAR THE LICENSE PLATE YOU'VE ALWAYS WANTED**

- EL - BRUTO - 1
- GOD - 61
- MISS - DIVA
- WARRIOR - 67
- AA - 001

- DAY 31 -

# MOOD CHART 1

I FEEL SATURN'S BELT TIGHTENING. IN A GOOD WAY

I FEEL LIKE STICKING A PRETTY, COLORFUL FEATHER INTO A BLACKBIRD'S TAIL

I DON'T FEEL HAPPY OR SAD. I FEEL LIKE A CLOUD THAT IS SLOWLY DISSOLVING

I FEEL LIKE RIPPING APART THIS BOOK, STEPPING ON IT, LIGHTING IT ON FIRE AND RUBBING THE REMAINING ASHES IN MY FACE

I COULD CRY OVER SOMETHING AS BIG AS THE COSMOS

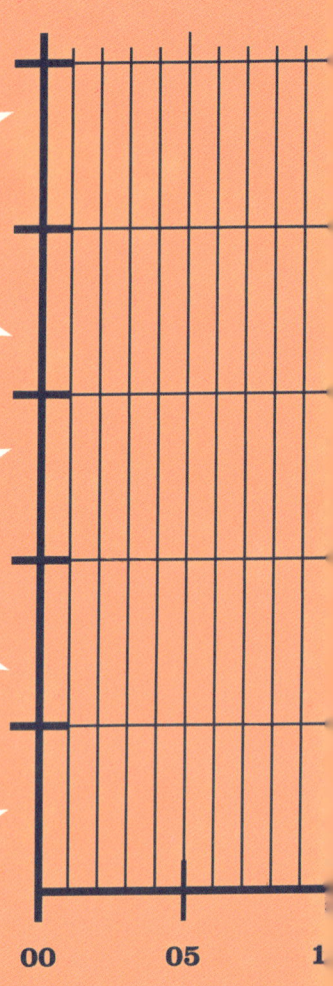

00    05    1

DAY

15  20  25  30

ND

2 MONTH

**JUMP IN A BOUNCY CASTLE**

- DAY 1 -

# SECRETLY TASTE CANDY IN AS MANY DRUG STORES AS POSSIBLE

- DAY 2 -

# ANSWER EACH AND EVERY EMAIL WITH A DRAWING

- DAY 3 -

CHEW BUBBLEGUM. THINK BIG. BLOW BUBBLES

- DAY 4 -

**ANSWER EVERY QUESTION WITH:**

**YES, I KNOW!**

- DAY 5 -

**SEARCH FOR HIDDEN MESSAGES IN YOUR MUSIC COLLECTION. PLAY THE RECORD BACKWARDS WHILE SEARCHING FOR CLUES IN THE PACKAGING AND THE NUMERICAL CODES**

- DAY 6 -

**MOONWALK ON EVERY ZEBRA CROSSING**

- DAY 7 -

**BUY ONE HUNDRED BOXES OF RAISINS AND SHARE THEM**

- DAY 8 -

# TAKE EVERYTHING VERY, VERY LITERALLY

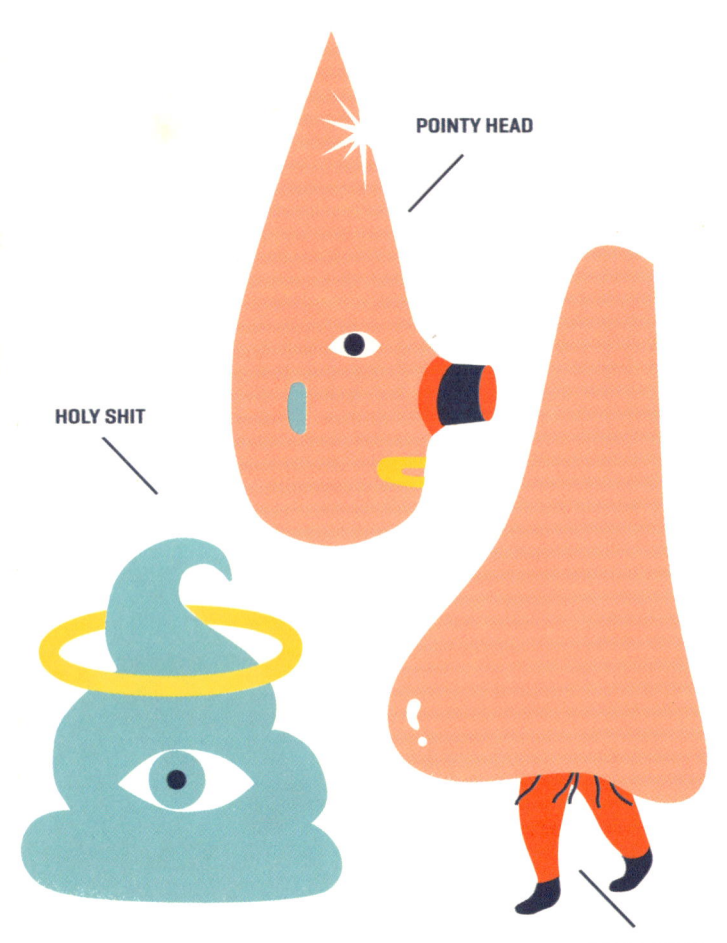

**POINTY HEAD**

**HOLY SHIT**

**RUNNY NOSE**

- DAY 9 -

**REPLACE ALL THE PASSWORDS ON YOUR COMPUTER WITH '123:HALLELUJAH!'**

*** **********

☐ REMEMBER MY PASSWORD

OK                            CANCEL

- DAY 10 -

**COUNT YOUR FARTS LIKE BLESSINGS**

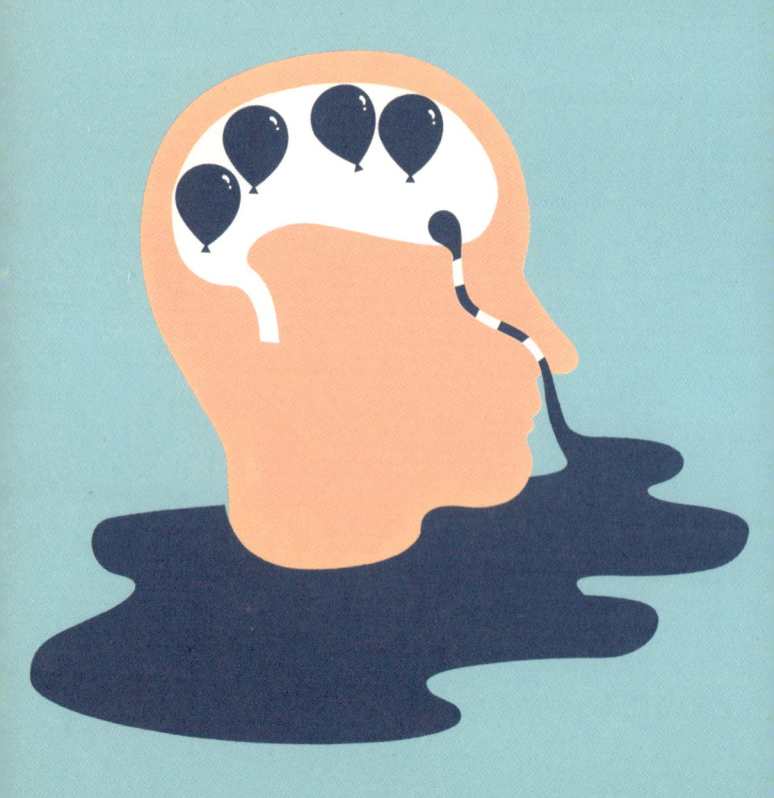

- DAY 11 -

# FINGER TAP 'GIBBERISH' IN MORSE CODE ON THE TABLE

- DAY 12 -

**CLIMB THE HIGHEST BUILDING IN YOUR NEIGHBORHOOD**

- DAY 13 -

MAKE UP A STRANGE OCCUPATION AND USE IT ON A NAMETAG

OFFICIAL TEACHER
**TWADDLE**

**ROUNDNESS INTRUCTOR**

**STABSTICK**
COACH

- DAY 14 -

# BUY 12 BOXES OF COLORED PENCILS AND FILL EACH BOX WITH 12 PENCILS OF THE SAME COLOR

- DAY 15 -

# START A NEW HOBBY

- [ ] **TOUCH YOUR RING FINGER WITH YOUR THUMB**
- [ ] **DISPOSE OF EXPLOSIVES**
- [ ] **CLICK YOUR TONGUE**
- [ ] **RECONSTRUCT EXTINCT KINDS OF PEANUT BUTTER**
- [ ] **HOPSCOTCH BACKWARDS**
- [ ] **PAINT FOOD**
- [ ] **HACK**

MAKE MINI GRAFFITI IN THE DARK WITH A SMALL WATERPROOF MARKER. MAKE TINY DRAWINGS, FOR EXAMPLE IN THE FURTHEST CORNER OF A BRICK - GRAFFITI YOU CAN ONLY SEE IF YOU LOOK VERY CLOSELY

- DAY 17 -

# CREATE YOUR OWN FAMILY COAT OF ARMS

- DAY 18 -

# DO EVERYTHING AS SILENTLY AS POSSIBLE

- DAY 19 -

**WALK INTO EVERY ROOM MIAMI VICE-STYLE**

- DAY 20 -

**RUN INTO A LAMP POST AS HARD AS YOU CAN**

- DAY 21 -

**IMAGINE YOURSELF AS A MAGIC MARKER AND DRAW AS MANY FLUID LINES AS POSSIBLE**

- DAY 22 -

**CREATE YOUR OWN FLAG OR HAVE SOMEONE MAKE IT FOR YOU. THEN HANG IT BECAUSE IT'S FLAG DAY**

- DAY 23 -

**MAKE A VIDEO OF BLENDING A BLENDER IN A BLENDER, AND THEN POST IT ON THE INTERNET**

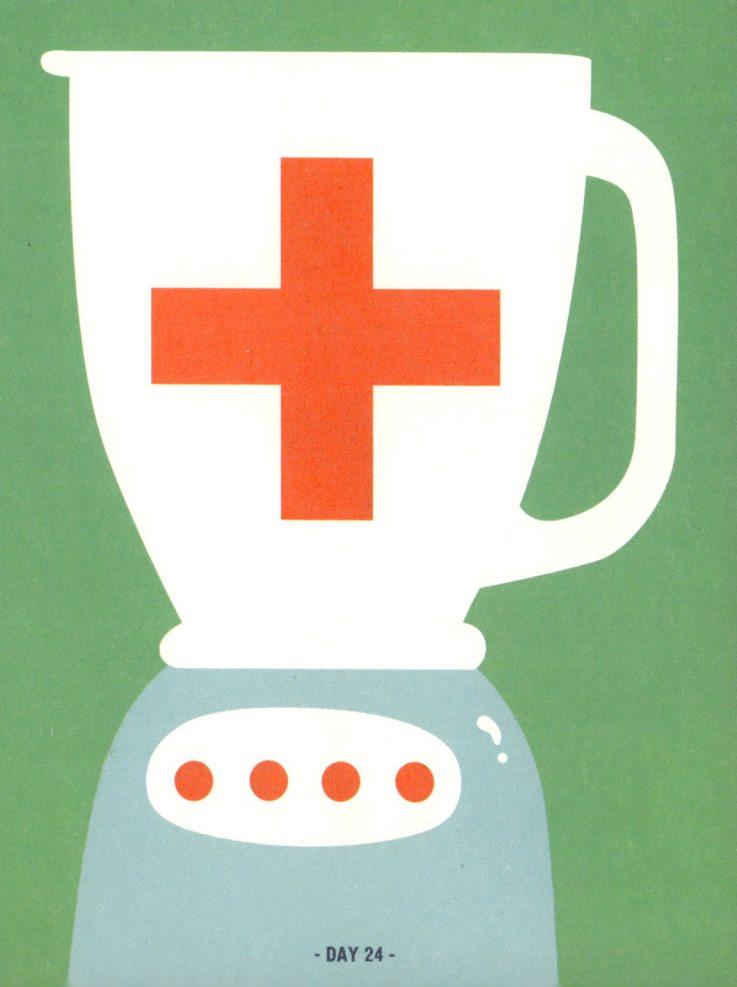

- DAY 24 -

**MAKE UP SOME FICTIONAL ADJECTIVES FOR CUTE LITTLE ANIMALS. CLOSE YOUR EYES AND VISUALISE THEM**

YOUNG DONGLING DOLPHIN

YOUNG NIPPILATING MOLE

- DAY 25 -

GET IN LINE FOR THE BANK MACHINE. WHENEVER SOMEONE LINES UP BEHIND YOU, GIVE HIM OR HER YOUR PLACE SO YOU ARE ALWAYS AT THE BACK OF THE LINE

302

- DAY 26 -

# START A NEW COLLECTION

- DAY 27 -

**PLAY WITH YOUR FOOD. BUILD A HOUSE MADE OUT OF BANANA SLICES, APPLE CUBES AND PEAR BRICKS. THEN EAT IT AS IF YOU'RE AN UNHOLY FRUIT MONSTER**

- DAY 28 -

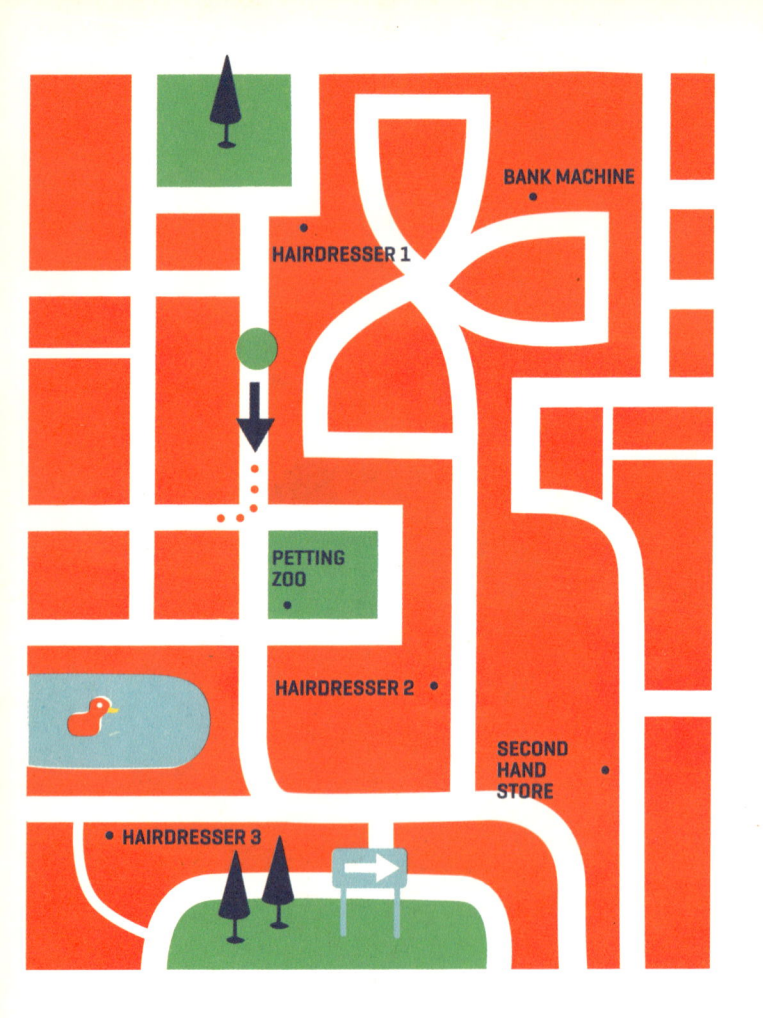

**WALK THROUGH TOWN USING THIS RULE: AFTER EACH RIGHT TURN, TAKE TWO LEFTS. KEEP THIS UP AS LONG AS POSSIBLE**

- DAY 29 -

**GO TO THE PETTING ZOO AND HUG AS MANY ANIMALS AS POSSIBLE**

- DAY 30 -

# MOOD CHART 2

IT'S SO PRETTY OUT HERE... EVERYTHING SEEMS TO FLOAT... AND THERE ARE SO MANY COLORS... THIS IS SO INTENSE

I FEEL LIKE A BABY HEDGEHOG WITH THE BRAIN OF STEPHEN HAWKING WHO JUST ATE A CHOCOLATE BAR

I FEEL LIKE AN OCTOPUS WITH 8 LEGS

I FEEL LIKE AN EMPTY BAG OF CHIPS FLOATING THROUGH SPACE

DARK METAL IS FOR SISSIES. EXCUSE ME WHILE I GO BLOW UP A CHURCH

00   05   10

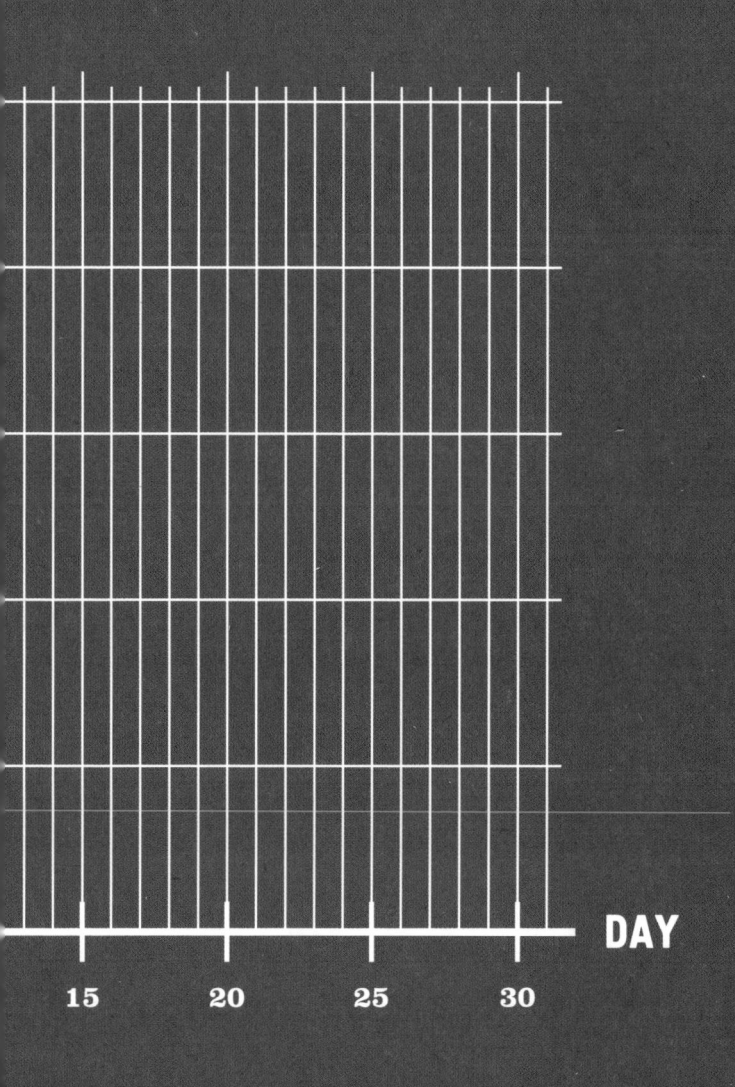

**DAY**

15  20  25  30

RD

# MONTH

**BUY A CHEAP PAINTING AT THE FLEA MARKET. PUT IT IN YOUR ROOM ON A CHAIR. TAKE A SHARP KNIFE. PACE THE ROOM UNTIL THE MOMENT ARRIVES. YOU WILL KNOW WHEN THE TIME IS RIGHT. THEN STAB INTO THE CANVAS WITH A FEW SHARP SLASHES**

**BUY A CREAM PIE, PUT IT ON THE TABLE AND DROP YOUR FACE IN IT**

- DAY 2 -

**FIND A CAR WITHOUT A PARKING TICKET AND BUY ONE FOR IT**

- DAY 3 -

# BREAK AS MANY WORLD RECORDS AS YOU CAN

**WORLD RECORD BUBBLEWRAP POPPING**

**WORLD RECORD GENERAL NON-VERBAL**

**WORLD RECORD ITCHY HEAD**

**WORLD RECORD PEANUT SALTING**

**WORLD RECORD MINDLESS AUTHORIZING**

**WORLD RECORD SEMI-AUTOMATIC BANANA PEELING**

- DAY 4 -

**CUT OUT BLACK SILHOUETTES AND STICK THEM ON TRAFFIC LIGHTS**

- DAY 5 -

**PUT YOUR LEG IN A CAST**

- DAY 6 -

# PLAN A DAY FULL OF BREAKS

**FLOATING BREAK**

**PLAY BREAK**

**FEAST BREAK**

**POLISH BREAK**

**SPORTS BREAK**

- DAY 7 -

**TAKE ADVANTAGE OF YOUR OWN INNOCENCE. FOR EXAMPLE: YOU CAN BUY A TRAIN TICKET. WHEN THE CONDUCTOR COMES TO ASK FOR YOUR TICKET, TRICK HIM WITH A TRANSPARENT EXCUSE. 'OHHH, I THOUGHT IT WAS A FREE TRAVEL DAY, BECAUSE OF IT BEING WORLD CONDUCTOR DAY.' OR 'ARE YOU BEING A RACIST?' ONCE THE CONDUCTOR STARTS ISSUING A FINE, TAKE OUT YOUR TICKET AND WAVE IT TRIUMPHANTLY IN HIS FACE**

# INVENT A TOILET CHOREOGRAPHY

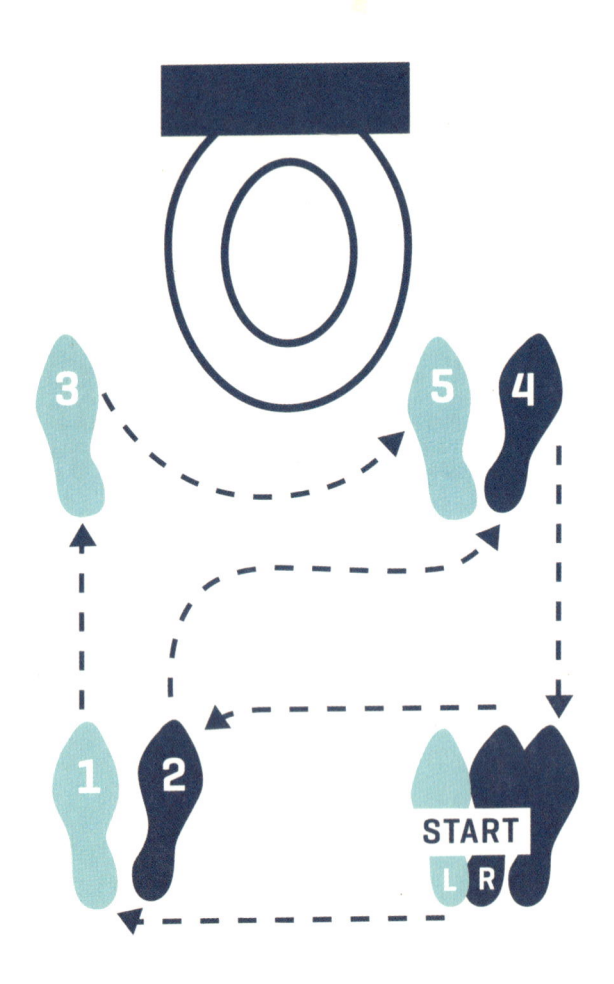

- DAY 9 -

# PLAY WITH SOAPY WATER

- DAY 10 -

# GO ON EBAY AND BUY AN 8MM FILM PROJECTOR AND A BOX OF 8MM FILMS

- DAY 11 -

**BUY A HAWAIIAN DICTIONARY AND TRY TO REPLACE THE WORDS YOU USE MOST WITH HAWAIIAN WORDS**

HUNGER - POLOLI
ANGRY - HUHU
FURIOUS - HUHU WELA LOA
INFURIATED - HUHU KAOHI'OLE
QUICK - WIKIWIKI
FOOD - 'AI
KISS - HO
KISS AGAIN - HONIHONI

# PIMP YOUR BIKE

- DAY 13 -

**OPEN A HOME RESTAURANT**

## TERRIFIC TRACY HAUTE CUISINE

### DISH OF THE DAY

QUICHE

HORSERADISH COMPOTE

STEWED PEARS GRANNY-STYLE

CHEESEBOARD WITH GRAPES

- DAY 14 -

**WALK BAREFOOT THROUGH THE GRASS**

- DAY 15 -

**WEAR CAMOUFLAGE WHILE GUARDING A LAKE OR TREE**

- DAY 16 -

# TAKE THINGS VERY SLOW

- DAY 17 -

**DON'T SAY:**

iON

YES!

- DAY 18 -

# MAKE A LIST OF THINGS YOU DON'T HAVE TO BECOME BECAUSE YOU ALREADY ARE THESE THINGS WITHOUT TRYING

- [ ] PIPSQUEAK
- [ ] GENERAL NON-EXPERT
- [ ] KNOW-IT-ALL
- [ ] BRAGGART
- [ ] PESSIMISM VIRTUOSO
- [ ] EXCELLENT HOPSCOTCHER
- [ ] MASTER OF HEAVY ACCENTS
- [ ] WIDESCREEN TV EXPERT
- [ ] HEAD OF EMPTY BATTERIES
- [ ] A GREEN MONSTER
- [ ] NEIGHBORHOOD SPY

**RE-INVENT A CLASSIC FASTFOOD RECIPE**

- DAY 20 -

# RENAME YOUR HOMETOWN

- DAY 21 -

**READ ALL BILLBOARDS OUT LOUD**

**JOHN'S AUDIOVISUALS**

**EXPRESS**

**MOTEL**

DOG GROOMER
**ONLY DOGS**

**FOX**
FOR THE LOVERS

- DAY 22 -

# ACT LIKE A CELEBRITY WHO DOESN'T WANT TO BE RECOGNISED

**A.**

**B.**

**C.**

A. PHOTOCOPY AT 800% AND CUT OUT
B. PHOTOCOPY AT 150% AND CUT OUT
C. PHOTOCOPY AT 300% AND CUT OUT

- DAY 23 -

# INTRODUCE YOURSELF TO SOMEONE YOU KNOW BY SIGHT BUT NEVER TALKED TO BEFORE

**SWIM UNDERWATER WITH YOUR EYES OPEN**

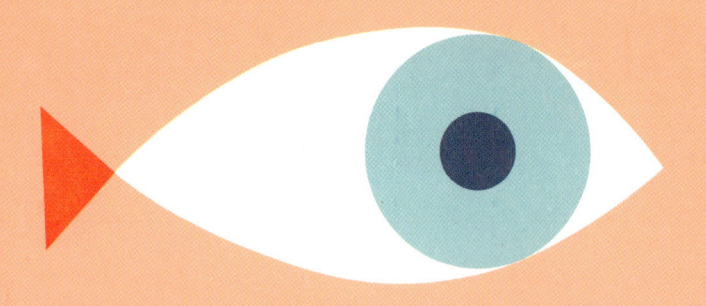

- DAY 25 -

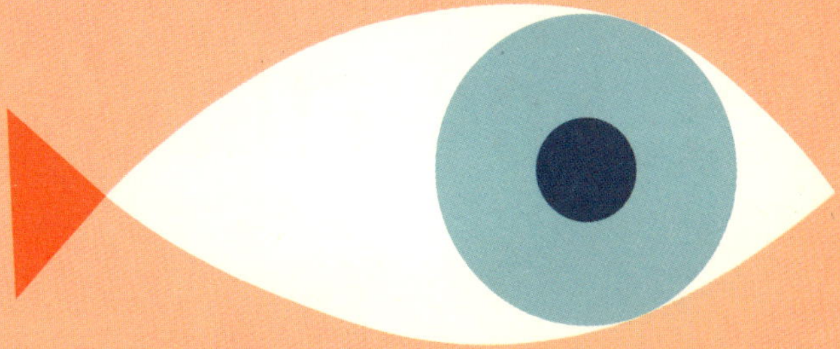

**ORGANIZE A PILLOW FIGHT**

▶ **INVITATION** ◀

# HUGE
## PILLOWFIGHT

**SUPER DUPER SOFT**

IT'S GOING DOWN AT MY PLACE!
TONIGHT: FANTASTICALLY FLUFFY,
LOTS OF FEATHERS
AND A GIANT BED...

COME IN YOUR PYJAMAS
BRING YOUR OWN PILLOW

**PLEASE COME!**

**DON'T FORGET YOUR FRIENDS**

- DAY 26 -

**WALK UP THE STAIRS BACKWARDS**

- DAY 27 -

**TRY TO THINK OF NOTHING UNTIL A THOUGHT COMES TO MIND.
WRITE THAT THOUGHT DOWN AND START OVER.
THEN ORGANIZE THEM UNDER THE FOLLOWING HEADINGS:**

**ANGRY**

**SECRET**

**MISERABLE**

**MOODY**

**JEALOUS**

**PETTY**

# TODAY IS WINK-DAY

ONE FOR THE CHICK

ONE FOR THE MOUSE

ONE FOR EACH CHILD

ONE FOR THE ANGRY NEIGHBOR

ONE FOR THE HARD WORKER

- DAY 29 -

**PAY YOUR BOSS A COMPLIMENT THAT YOU'VE NEVER MADE BEFORE**

- WHAT AN AMAZINGLY COOL TIE!
- THAT MOUSTACHE LOOKS REALLY GREAT ON YOU!
- I LOVE HOW YOU USE THIS SPACE
- YOU CAN BE ABSENT-MINDED IN A GREAT WAY

**ONLY EAT THINGS THAT CONTAIN CHOCOLATE**

- DAY 31 -

# MOOD CHART 3

I'LL HAVE SOME MORE OF THAT

I FEEL LIKE A FAT LAZY CAT CHILLING IN THE SUN

FEELINGS ARE NOTHING MORE THAN CHEMICALS IN YOUR BRAIN AND ALL THE CHEMICALS HAVE DISAPPEARED

I FEEL LIKE AN OLD MOLE WITHOUT GLASSES

I BURIED MY LAPTOP

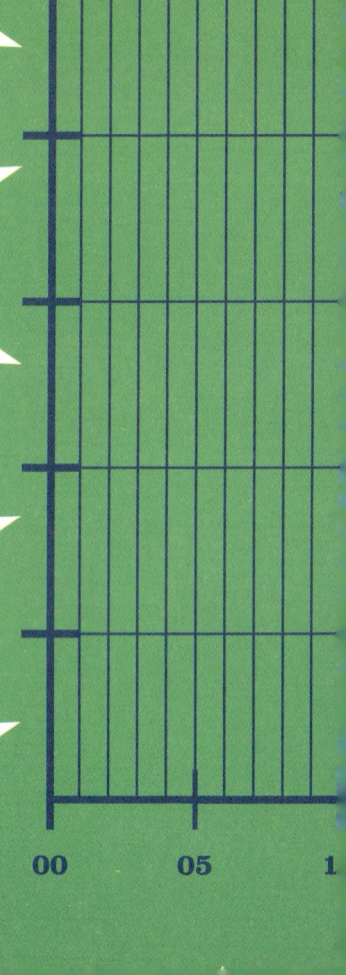

00    05    1

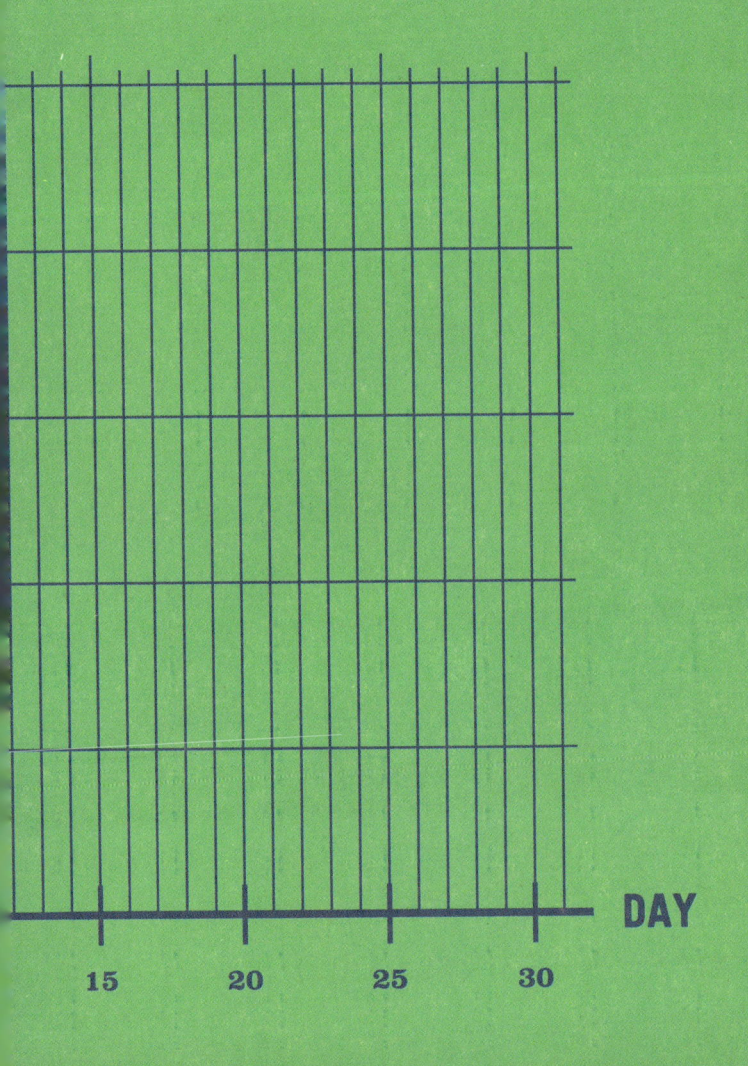

**DAY**

15  20  25  30

3 1/2

# MONTHS

# LOOK UP

- DAY 1 -

**ALSO DURING THE DAYTIME**

- DAY 2 -

**PAY YOURSELF A COMPLIMENT**

> I'M SO GOOD AT PAYING COMPLIMENTS TO MYSELF!

- DAY 3 -

**01** TAKE A BIG PILE OF OLD MAGAZINES, LEAFLETS AND NEWSPAPERS

**02** CUT OUT AS MANY COMMAS, PERIODS AND OTHER PUNCTUATION MARKS AS YOU CAN FIND

**03** MAKE A NICE COLLAGE

**04** FRAME YOUR COLLAGE AND PUT IT ON THE WALL

- DAY 4 -

**COLOR THE COVER OF THIS BOOK**

# CHEERFUL
## IN 3½ MONTHS

- DAY 5 -

**NO ANTI-DEPRESSANTS ALLOWED**

- DAY 6 -

# HAPPY PILLS

**CONTAINS NOSHITANDURINEPOOPHOLE**

SWALLOW 1 EACH DAY
WATCH OUT! CAN CAUSE HALLUCINATIONS

YEAR 1918

50 TABLETS

**COPY THIS TAG AND STICK IT TO A BOTTLE OF VITAMIN C.
ENJOY THE PLACEBO EFFECT**

- DAY 7 -

# LIFT UP A PAVING STONE AND IDENTIFY ALL THE BUGS YOU SEE

- DAY 8 -

**WHILE ON YOUR WAY HOME ON THE BUS OR SUBWAY GET OUT ONE STOP TOO LATE, WALK BACK AND DISCOVER THINGS YOU NORMALLY WOULD NOT SEE**

- DAY 9 -

**SAY NOTHING IN AS MANY WAYS AS POSSIBLE**

- BAD BREATH IS BETTER THAN NO BREATH AT ALL
- YOU'RE ALL THUMBS
- LOST TIME IS NEVER FOUND
- IT'S A HARD NUT TO CRACK
- THAT'S JUST THE WAY IT IS
- COME RAIN OR SHINE

- DAY 10 -

**FIND A PRETTY PEBBLE AND PRESENT IT WITH AN AWARD**

- DAY 11 -

**FOLLOW A PERSON WHO IS OBVIOUSLY NOT GUILTY OF ANYTHING**

- DAY 12 -

**USE THE WORD MAGNETOPHONE AS CASUALLY AS POSSIBLE**

> SO I MAGNETOPHONE TO HIM THAT MAGNETOPHONE SHOULD HAVE MAGNETOPHONED THAT MAGNETOPHONE A WHOLE MAGNETOPHONE EARLIER

- DAY 13 -

**DON'T DO ANYTHING**

- DAY 14 -

# MOOD CHART 3½

- I FEEL LIKE A BANK MACHINE GONE WILD
- I FEEL LIKE A CHILD WHO CUT A BUTTERFLY OUT OF PAPER
- I FEEL LIKE A LINE RUNNING PARALLEL TO A STRIPE
- I FEEL LIKE A GIRAFFE WITH A SORE NECK
- I'M GOING TO BLOW UP A BUDDHA STATUE

00   05   1

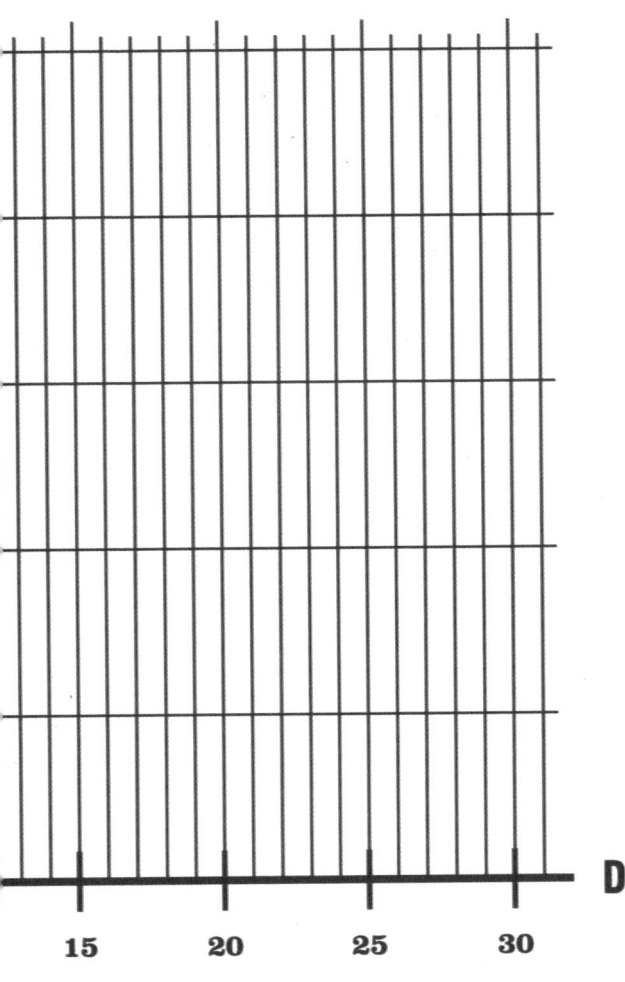

DAY

15  20  25  30

# ACKNOWLEDGEMENTS

We thank the robins, the roll of toilet paper that was there after all, the 50-dollar bill that came swirling out of a book and the firelighters that keep us warm. And our neighbors.

| | |
|---|---|
| Concept | Uitgeverij Snor |
| Illustrations | Sue Doeksen |
| Text | Gerard Janssen |
| Translation | Steve Korver, Pien van Ooijen |
| Design | Rick Storm |
| Lay-out | En Publique |

ISBN: 978-90-79961-12-2
NUR: 370
©Uitgeverij Snor, Utrecht, the Netherlands

All rights reserved. No part of this publication may be reproduced, stored in a retrieval system, or transmitted, in any form or by any means, electronic, mechanical, photocopying, recording or otherwise, without the prior permission of the publishers.

'Cheerful!' is a publication of Uitgeverij Snor. This book has been prepared with great care. The authors and the employees of Uitgeverij Snor accept no liability for any inaccuracies, nor do we accept any liability for any loss resulting from inaccuracies in, and/or incompleteness of this publication.

**Did you receive 'Cheerful' but still feel depressed?**
**Please contact:**
**Uitgeverij Snor**
**Hooghiemstraplein 15**
**3514 AX Utrecht**
**The Netherlands**
**www.uitgeverijsnor.nl**
**Info@uitgeverijsnor.nl**